# ReadyGEN
# Text Collection

W9-BID-941

**SAVVAS**
LEARNING COMPANY

ISBN-13: 978-0-328-85275-8
ISBN-10:    0-328-85275-9

10 2021

# Planting for the Future

4

# THE FAMILY TREE

## BY
## DAVID McPHAIL

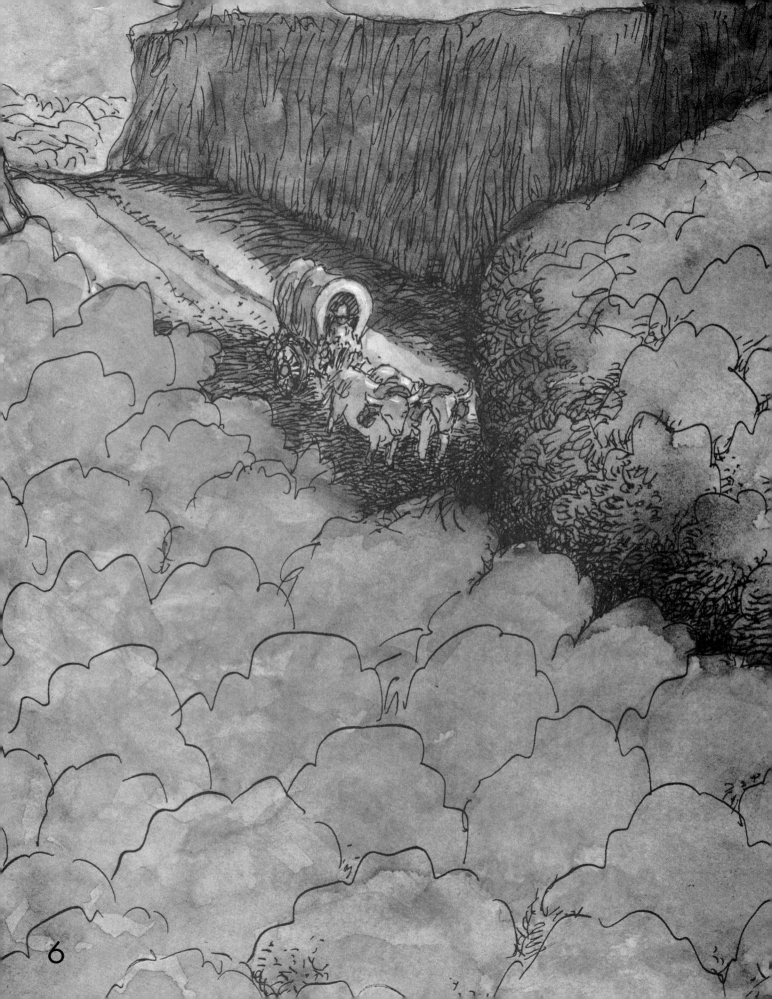

Many years ago, a young man came to the wilderness to start a new life.

He chopped down trees to make fields for his crops and pastures for his animals.

But he left one tree standing. It would provide shade for his house during the long hot summers and act as a buffer against the chilly winter winds.

The man used the logs to make boards
and beams for his house and barns.

He used others to make posts and rails
for his fences.

He and his oxen removed the tree
stumps and dragged them to the edges
of the fields.

CREEAAK

Then the man built his house.
When it was finished, he went away.

Weeks later, he returned with his wife.

Eventually, they had a child. A son.

After a while, more people came.
Now the family had neighbors.

Years passed. The man grew old.

His son took over the running of
the farm, and he had a son of his own
to help him.

New generations joined the family.
Old ones left. The tree witnessed it all.

Now, the great-great-grandson of the
first settler lived on the farm. The boy
loved the tree. It was like a friend to him.

One day, workers came to widen
the road to make room for more cars,
more trucks.

The tree was in the way—it would
have to come down.

The boy protested. He stood
between the workers and tree, and
would not budge.

A call for assistance went out.

Help soon arrived.

The boy and his dog were not alone.

The workers huddled. They devised
a new plan—one that would work for
everyone.

# The Life Cycle of an Apple Tree

## by Linda Tagliaferro

# Apple Seeds

How do apple trees grow?

Apple trees grow

from tiny apple seeds.

You can find apple seeds

inside apples.

Apple seeds need sunlight, soil, water and warmth. Then they sprout and grow.

# Growing

Apple trees have one main
stem called the trunk.
Branches grow on the trunk.
Leaves cover the tree.

After three years,

flower buds form

and open in summer.

Apple blossoms fill

the whole tree.

Parts of the flower blossoms
turn into fruit.
The little green apples keep
growing bigger.
Seeds form inside.

# Apples!

Apples grow all summer
and turn red in fall.
They are ripe
and ready to be picked.

Some apples fall
to the ground.
They rot and the seeds
come out.

# Starting Over

Next year, new apple trees
can grow from the seeds.
The life cycle continues.

# How Apple Trees Grow

seeds

young tree

blossoms

apples

# Glossary

**life cycle**—the stages in the life of a plant that include growing, reproducing, and dying

**seed**—the part of a flowering plant that can grow into a new plant

**soil**—the dirt where plants grow; most plants get their food and water from the soil.

**sprout**—to grow, appear, or develop quickly; sprouting seeds produce roots and stems.

**stem**—the long main part of a plant that makes leaves

**trunk**—the main stem of a tree

# GARDEN TIP

## by George Shannon

To grow enough to eat all year,
your seeds must be tiptop.
So plant both ends of old toy cars
and have a bumper crop!

# DANCING IN THE BREEZE
## by George Shannon

I went to the garden
to pick some peas.
Found them dancing
in the evening breeze.

The day was hot,
so I joined right in.
Tapped my toes
and began to grin.

Peppers in a polka
as the snow peas snapped.
Beans in a boogie
as the cabbage clapped.

Squash square dancing
with a cha-cha chard.
Watermelon waltzing
all around the yard.

Picked my supper
with the greatest ease—
everything swinging
in the dancing breeze.

# ZUCCHINI

**by George Shannon**

Zucchini
meeny
miney
moe.
Plant a seed
and watch it grow.

Eeny
meeny
makes a lot.
Like a magic
cooking pot.

Eeny
meeny
munch a lot.
Zucchini every meal—
you've got:

62

Zucchini bread.
Zucchini spread.
Zucchini casseroles.

Zucchini pies.
Zucchini fries.
Zucchini dinner rolls.

Zucchini juice.
Zucchini mousse.
Zucchini jam and scone.

Zucchini hash
and succotash.
Zucchini
meeny
miney

MOAN.